Around the World
in
Fifteen Friends

Dedicated to the people in the stories,
and to everyone else who has made
my travels so interesting.

Introduction
Written in Melbourne

Over the past eight years I've traveled to six continents to visit over seventy countries, some of them many times. I've seen some of the wonders of the world like the pyramids, Macchu Picchu, and the Great Wall, and have experienced astounding nature like the mountains of China, the laurel forest of Madeira, and the desert of northern Chile.

I've benefited greatly by seeing the world. Seeing great human triumphs alongside the indescribable beauty of nature has inspired me to achieve more while simultaneously imbuing me with a deep gratitude merely for being on this earth.

But most important by far have been the people I've met along the way. I've seen human nature firsthand from many angles and have come to understand the human experience slightly better.

There's a common worry that the world is becoming a hostile and dangerous place. And certainly some areas of the world are, at times, those things. But my fellow travelers and I all take a much more optimistic view of the world.

The world is full of good people trying to do the right thing. I've been the recipient of a stranger's kindness more times than I can count. The times I've experienced hostility have been few and far between, and I haven't exactly been careful to avoid those situations.

I've tried to include a variety of stories, from those that are amusing trifles along with those that have shown me the depths of human kindness.

I hope that by reading my stories you are reminded of the goodness in the people in your life, both those at home and those who you've met while away from home. And if you aren't a fellow traveler, maybe I can provide a small nudge towards getting out there and seeing what the world is all about.

Some of the people in this book are now my closest friends. Others I met once and will never see again. But through my interactions with all of them I have learned about the world and myself, and have become a better person. I'm more grateful for that than for all of the things I've seen.

Charlie – Boston
Written in Israel

Our school was abuzz with the news. It was a small school, only eighty-one people in my grade, so information always spread quickly. We were getting a foreign student, a kid from Taiwan who didn't speak any English.

I knew a thing or two; I was a fifth grader, after all. Taiwan was basically China, which was in Asia, and that's where ninjas came from. And I'd always wanted to be a ninja, so I was naturally pretty interested in this news. I would teach this kid English, he would teach me Chinese, and then I'd be one step closer to becoming a ninja.

The logic doesn't stand up to the test of time, but it seemed sound back then.

And as it turned out, that's pretty much how it happened. Not the ninja part, but I did help him learn English and he helped me learn Chinese. I taught him that bugle isn't pronounced "buggle", and he taught me how to swear in Chinese. Eventually my curses required different pronouns, so I had to learn those, and soon I could have basic conversations. Thanks to him and his family I speak with very little accent, which seems to give Chinese people the impression that I must understand far more than I actually do.

Up until this point in my life I had never been on a plane. I'd taken road trips as far as New York or Vermont, but had never left the country. I'm not sure I really even thought about going on plane trips. You can imagine my excitement when Charlie and his family invited me to visit Taiwan with them for a month over the summer of sixth grade.

My parents wouldn't allow it, which seemed ridiculously unfair.

The offer was repeated after seventh grade, and they cautiously agreed to let me go. I would fly to Taiwan with Charlie, his family, and our other friend Ryan, and then I'd fly back all by myself.

Many precautions were taken. My parents got passports in case they needed to come rescue me. I got a lot of immunizations that I now think may have been unnecessary. I was given motion-sickness medicine. And I overpacked to the point that I had the boardgame Stratego in case I got bored on the plane and could convince someone to play with me. I was prepared, but more importantly, my parents were prepared to let me go.

Charlie was an excellent basketball player, and towered over the rest of us at five-feet seven, a height he boasts to this day. We would go play basketball with the locals, who were equally in awe him. They yelled out compliments/insults like, "Michael Jo Jo Man" and "Banana to your brother!", the latter of which I still mutter under my breath from time to time.

At the time I looked a lot like Macaulay Culkin, which was a cool thing because Home Alone was a very popular movie amongst my peers and he hadn't yet succumbed to the destructive power of drugs. The likeness was so striking that a Masai warrior once stopped a school assembly that he was hosting to single me out and ask if I was indeed The Culkin.

I'm not sure if it was my likeness to Macaulay, or just the fact that I was one of very few foreigners who visited Taiwan, but I was treated like a celebrity. Everyone waved to me, some gawked, many took photos. When we visited the science museum, an entire class field trip took to following us around taking pictures and fully encircling our table two-deep as we ate in the McDonald's in the museum.

McDonalds, by the way, was just about the only food I would eat. His family prepared all sorts of dishes that I now recognize as delicious, but

I was such a picky eater that all I wanted was my McDonalds Filet-O-Fish.

After two weeks, Ryan couldn't handle it anymore. He was homesick. We had a very solemn goodbye where he handed me his economy pack of cream-filled oatmeal cookie sandwiches.

"You're going to need these more than I will."

I'm so grateful to have been brought to Asia so young. I don't think I fully understood at the time just how generous it was for Charlie and his family to take me there, and how brave it was of my parents to let me go. Charlie and I became even better friends than before, I felt like a second son to their family, and I can't help but think that the seed of international travel was planted there. Maybe my trip with Charlie is the reason I travel everywhere, but always come back to Asia.

Todd – Austin, Texas
Written in Rome

I didn't meet Todd while traveling, but he has been so instrumental to many of these stories, and the fact that I travel in the first place, that there's no way to write this book without talking about him a little bit.

Todd and I met in college, as many friends do. We both lived in a private dorm that made the tactical mistake of trying to isolate potential troublemakers by putting them on the higher floors. They never considered that maybe those troublemakers would become friends and become better, or worse, than the sum of their parts.

We found ourselves breaking into the roof of the twenty-seven story building, riding on the top of the elevators, and refinishing the doors on our floor after a vigorous round of "golf darts", a sport which we invented.

Todd is the sort of guy who is so kind and empathetic that you are forced to confront the idea that maybe you aren't such a great person after all. He's also completely self-sufficient, a good conversationalist, and up for just about any adventure. In other words, he's the perfect travel companion.

We first traveled together a few years after we left college, him by graduating, me by dropping out. We both worked at a small tech company called Smiley Media in downtown Austin, Texas. One day after work, we were waiting in the office for a movie that started in an hour. Todd asked if I had ever seen the video of "Dancing Matt", a guy who traveled all around the world and danced in every place he visited. He then spliced the video together to create a short video of him dancing all over the world.

"Doesn't watching that make you want to travel?" he asked.

It did. This was my first job, and it seemed like I ought to use those vacation days to which I was entitled.

"How about if we agree to book a trip to another country before we leave for the movie?"

We shook hands in agreement and started looking online. Both of us relatively untraveled, we had no idea where we'd even want to go. After burning fifteen precious minutes we narrowed our options down to Tokyo or Istanbul. We hadn't been to either, both seemed exotic, and there were special deals on each for around the same price.

A coin was flipped, it landed on tails, and both of our lives were changed permanently. We booked our tickets immediately with plenty of time left to go to the movie.

We bought a train pass for three hundred dollars. That seemed like a lot of money for a metro system, but we knew that Japan was expensive. That was about all we knew about Japan, which was the whole point; we wanted an adventure.

The room we booked was in Asakusa, Tokyo. The area is a little bit on the outskirts of the Tokyo core and is too touristy to qualify as a must-do, but we didn't know that at the time. We arrived at Narita airport, took the train into the city, and emerged from Asakusa station. It was raining and foggy, and we happened to emerge from the exit that deposits you right in front of Senso-ji, the temple in Asakusa.

Senso-ji is everything you'd expect from a Japanese temple. It's red, huge, and looks Japanese in every way. A giant rice paper lantern hangs from the main arch. We were blown away. Japan was so foreign and so interesting. It was everything we had hoped it would be.

I think that's the moment I fell in love with traveling.

We went to the train office to trade our order confirmation for our actual train pass and had the rules explained to us. The pass worked on the main loop around Tokyo, but it also worked on bullet trains and regional trains that spanned the entire country. We had accidentally bought the country-wide train pass.

That week was the first of our great travel adventures. We traveled all over the country and saw places as different from those at home as two places could get. Our worlds had expanded, and the love at first sight with international travel was quickly cemented. When we got back my boss explained to me that you have to tell your employer in advance when you are taking vacation. You can't just leave. I quit soon after that.

A year later we sat with a few others in a friend's apartment, playing a game of Risk. If you haven't played Risk before, it's a board game that's played on a world map. All night long we moved our pieces across the world to places we had never been.

A thought had been brewing in my mind for the preceding few weeks. I thought of myself as someone who was worldly and adventurous, but my trips since Japan had been nearby. Vegas, New York, maybe the Caribbean. But some people, like dancing Matt, traveled all the time.

Why wasn't I doing that?

I looked out at the map we were playing on, at all of the countries I'd never seen before. My life wasn't on track to see any of those places. Maybe I should change that.

"I'm going to sell all of my stuff and live around the world for a while. Maybe forever."

I said it with more certainty than I expected. Todd thought for a minute or two and said, "Good idea. I'll go with you."

By the next day we chose a date, January 6th, 2008. No matter what, we would leave on that day. It gave us two months to prepare. We sold our valuables and invited people on the internet to come scavenge the rest. Soon we had nothing beyond a couple of outfits and toiletries.

At the same time, we geared up for our trip. We went to a local travel and outdoor gear store and surveyed the backpacks. I wanted to get a big one, but Todd pushed for twenty-eight liter backpacks that looked barely larger than school backpacks. I told him they were way too small, but he insisted that they would be enough.

On January sixth we had our little bags packed to the brim, but were confident that we had enough to keep us going. In one of the pockets we each had a stack of tickets that would take us to Central America, Asia, the Middle East, and Europe. We both had lists of places we wanted to go, and we bartered with each other to come up with the itinerary. Some stops were for just a few days, but most were for a month or two. We didn't have a ticket that brought us back to the United States at the end.

Todd and I both travel independently now, but we still go on a lot of trips together. This year alone we went on three round-the-world trips in a row. We've never once had a fight, or even a disagreement that caused one of us to raise his voice. Considering the occasional stress and uncertainty of travel, especially with two guys who aren't afraid to get into a lot of trouble, that's an enormous credit to Todd's character.

Oyden and Ory - Panama
Written in Messina, Sicily

The first stop on our inaugural trip was to Panama City, Panama. It was one of the places that I pushed for, but I don't remember why anymore. I think it had something to do with my impression of the city, which was that it was well developed, but a little bit rough. Costa Rica sounded like the kind of place yoga girls would go to eat mangoes on the beach, but Panama sounded like the kind of place where we'd find adventure, and maybe a little bit of trouble.

First, though, we had a stopover in Houston, Texas where we used our credit cards to get into the United airport lounge for free. One of our goals on the trip was to keep up our vegan diet and our Crossfit workout routine. The lounge didn't have much food that we could eat, but there was plenty of open space for a workout.

In preparation for the trip Todd bought a good quality video camera and I bought a good quality still camera. He set the video camera up on a nearby chair to record our workout, eager to start the flow of funny videos back to our friends and family.

We did push-ups, sit-ups, squats, and burpees. A few people in the lounge were intrigued, but most of the suited businessmen weren't particularly impressed. That increased our own amusement. After half an hour we finished the workout and used the luxe showers in the lounge to wash our gym clothes and clean off.

We liked Panama immediately. On our first night we got to play poker in a casino where we were propositioned by prostitutes who wrote their phone numbers on the back of Catholic prayer cards. We settled into a private room at a hostel and quickly found three different vegan restaurants, each being very high quality and very inexpensive.

The restaurant nearest to our hostel was called Mireya's. It was run by a friendly woman named Mireya as well as her boyfriend, Jorge. Jorge was old and nearly deaf, always wore those four-pocket Cuban shirts, and was a lawyer. He recognized us either by our voices or our stilted Spanish and would chat with us every day at lunch. We didn't really understand what he was saying.

Carnival was approaching. Rio de Janeiro is, of course, the world center for Carnival, but we were told that Panama had the second biggest celebration. A major highway in Panama City was shut down to create an area for concerts, street food, and general mayhem. Later in our trip it was the site of a riot, which, from the news coverage, didn't seem that different from Carnival.

Jorge repeated himself several times before we understood that he was asking what our plans were for Carnival. We answered, but it was clear that he wasn't really interested in our answer. He wanted to suggest somewhere. We couldn't understand what he was saying, so he went and got a piece of paper. On it it said:

Carnival
Las Tablas
Go

Fair enough. We looked it up on the map and it was a tiny town in the middle of nowhere, which suited us just fine. More than partying and reveling, we wanted adventure. That's why we had come to Panama in the first place.

Our four-hour drive from Panama City to Las Tablas was more lively than we would have expected. Tourism in Panama was pretty sparse at the time, especially to the interior. Sometimes people cheered and high-fived, other times they gave us the finger. They were smiling in either case, so we took both equally as signs of affection.

Las Tablas was, indeed, a tiny little town. At its center is a square, which served as the venue for the Carnival festivities. Despite its small size, the celebration was absolutely out of control. The square was packed with parade floats with huge bands, all playing at the same time. Fireworks were shot off constantly at such low altitudes that the shrapnel from them constantly rained on the crowds. People flooded the streets and walked with the parade, in between the floats. This wasn't your typical orderly American celebration.

The story, we learned, was that there were two competing factions in the town, north street and south street. All year round, through the stores on those streets each group would collect donations for their Carnival festivities. Then, at the same time, both streets would try to outdo each other, creating a chaotic and incredible scene.

We joined the revelers in the streets, and I was even allowed to dance around with the flag and lead the parade of one of the streets. It was the most Panamanian I've ever felt. Everyone was happy and accepted us, even though we stuck out like sore thumbs.

Taking a break from the parade, we walked into the center of the square where things were just slightly less hectic. We sat down on a step to eat some apples we had bought from a convenience store. Soon after we were approached by two guys.

They each stood over six feet tall and were in perfect shape. Their tank tops revealed enormous muscles.

"Hey, we know you."

I didn't know anyone in Panama at that point, especially not in the interior. I was certain that we were about to be mugged or kidnapped.

"Oh, no, I don't think so. Wrong person."

"No. We know you."

"Sorry, I don't think you do."

"Yes we do. We know you."

Their insistence was intimidating. We clearly didn't know them, but they weren't going to go away. We were scared, and it probably showed.

"We saw your video on YouTube. The one where you were doing burpees in the airport."

Quickly they transformed from possible assailants to friendly faces. With only a couple hundred views, how was it possible that two random guys from Panama had happened to see our video, and then recognize us in the middle of nowhere?

We learned that their families were political entities in Panama, and that they themselves worked in government. But their passion was fitness and they wanted to start the first ever Crossfit gym in Panama.

We became fast friends. We ate meals together and did Crossfit workouts in playgrounds at night. They opened their gym a year or so later and it was so successful that they quickly had to move to a larger space. Two years later we came back to Panama and spent Carnival with them and their families.

Panpan – Beijing, China
Written in the Persian Gulf

It was my first time in China and only barely qualified as a visit. I was heading to Tokyo but had managed to book a flight that had a twenty-four hour stop in Beijing on the way there and a similar stop in Shanghai on the way back.

The plane landed late at night. Outside was so smoggy that every light source at the airport, both inside and out, projected a cone in the mist of pollutants suspended in the air. I descended into the subway system, transferred once, and climbed the stairs up to Beijing.

I expected a metropolis, but it was more of a sprawl. Electric scooters silently zoomed everywhere, mostly by way of the sidewalks. Tall buildings rose in every direction, their names emblazoned in illuminated Chinese characters. That's when I realized that I knew my hotel's name in English, but not in Chinese. After a brief panic I realized that my Kindle could connect to the internet in any country, so I used it to (very slowly) find a map of where the hotel was.

My hotel was typical of an inexpensive luxury hotel in China, which is to say that it was well decorated, very comfortable, and ever-so-slightly incorrectly built. In this case the bathroom had a large unusable space between one side of the glass shower and the wall. I got the impression that it was supposed to be built against the wall, but the water connection wasn't quite right so they improvised.

I went to sleep almost immediately. My stopover was so short that I really only had time for one thing, and I wanted to go see the Forbidden City the next morning.

The forbidden city is an extraordinary palace complex in the center of Beijing that served as living quarters for the royal families for almost five hundred years. It's guarded by a wall so thick that walking through it is like walking through a tunnel. Inside the thirty-foot-long tunnel are hustlers trying to sell you things that you definitely don't want.

Near the end of the tunnel, a woman jumped in front of me and tried to give me a small Chinese flag. It was a thin printed piece of plastic fastened to a straw as the flagpole. Estimated retail value: approximately one penny. No thank you, I said in Chinese. She insisted. I refused again. She insisted again. No thank you. She placed it into my hand, implying that it was a gift. Thank you, I said, and started to walk away. Then, of course, she demanded money. I tried to hand the flag back, but she wouldn't take it. I placed it on a ledge in the tunnel, which caused her to yell at me and start following me.

Suddenly I felt someone grab my hand. It couldn't be her, as she was on my other side. I looked over and saw a cute Chinese woman a few years younger than me holding my hand. Come on, she said in bad English.

We reached the end of the tunnel and stepped into the smog-filtered sun. We introduced ourselves. Her name was Panpan. Through our introduction we realized that neither my Chinese nor her English were particularly strong. After a little bit of chat we somehow discovered that we both spoke Spanish, so that became our default language, shifting to English or Chinese only when necessary.

I was immediately suspicious of Panpan. Just a week prior I had listened to a podcast where the narrator talking about meeting a young attractive woman in Beijing and being suckered into buying "art". Predictably, Panpan told me that she was an art student.

I'm not one to shy away from awkward situations, though, and knew that no amount of beguiling would convince me to buy her art. I decided that I would string her along, act oblivious to her ploy, and at least get some entertainment from the situation.

She told me that she was from a small village, and that this was her first time in Beijing. Of course it is, I thought. I bet it's your first time here every single day. Despite claiming to be new here, she knew everything there was to know about the Forbidden City. In fact, she was a rather excellent tour guide.

When I asked how a first-timer knew so much, she explained that every student in China learned about the Forbidden City in school. But do they really remember the details of the rainwater drainage system? It felt like a stretch.

And, of course, there was a small art gallery in the middle of the Forbidden City. Maybe I wanted to go look? No, thank you. Oh, but it's such great art! We browsed the art, and I was surprised when she allowed me to leave without resistance.

I was even more surprised when she stuck by my side afterwards. If she wasn't trying to get a commission on art, she must be on an even longer con. I wondered what it was. My kidneys tensed in nervous anticipation.

She seemed genuinely excited to have befriended a foreigner. She was good. She called one of her friends and had him talk to me for a few minutes to practice his English. Maybe she'd suggest we meet later and he would be the one to harvest my kidney?

It was cold, and she noticed that my hands were cold. She took one of her purple knitted mittens off of her hand and gave it to me. We would each have one warm hand and one cold one. I thought at the time that that might have been one of the sweetest gestures anyone had ever paid me. Very clever, very manipulative.

We spent hours walking around the Forbidden City. It's quite a site to see, from the preserved palace rooms, to the beautiful statues, to the gardens within. Once we'd seen enough, we walked out together. She pointed at a big museum across the way, saying that we must see it. I agreed, but she told me that they don't allow backpacks. We could go one by one, each watching the other's backpack. Way too obvious of a scam for me to fall for, I demurred.

The one other thing on my list to do was to eat Peking duck. You have to buy an entire duck, which is enough to feed four, for around $50. I was going to do it alone, so I figured I may as well invite her to join me. She agreed and we went to a place nearby that she recommended.

We ordered the duck and continued talking as we ate it. She told me about her village and showed me her passport. Sure enough, she was from where she claimed to be from. Was it possible that she wasn't somehow trying to con me?

The duck was delicious, and proved to be far more than we could eat together. The bill came, and I pulled out my wallet to pay for it.

Surprisingly, she also reached for her wallet and came up with half of the money.

Surely if she was ready to pay for her half, she wasn't scamming me. I was shocked. She knew that I was about to leave, and that we'd never see each other, but she still wanted to pay for her half?

I insisted, saying that I had planned on buying the duck whether she was there or not, so her half hadn't really cost me anything. But she would not allow me to pay for her. She eventually put her half of the money in front of me and said that if I didn't take it, she would just leave it there. I believed her and eventually took it.

We left the restaurant as actual friends, not a genuinely sweet Chinese girl and a suspicious American. She waited with me in the train station until I absolutely had to leave. On the wall was a big mosaic mural of the world. We talked about the places I'd been and the places she wanted to go. I wished that I could just whisk her away to Europe or something, just to pay her back for her kindness, and to make up for secretly questioning her every move.

We exchanged email addresses, but writing in a mash of Chinese, Spanish, and English was so frustrating that the emails became shorter and less frequent until they vanished entirely. I still think about her every once in a while and wonder if she got to travel to any of those places she wanted to see. When she does, I hope she meets a nice stranger who acts as a tour guide for her, too.

Carl - Dominican Republic
Written in Crete

A year after we began traveling, Todd needed a break from life in the sky. Only in retrospect will he admit that it had a lot to do with a girl back home that he'd begun spending time with in between trips. I wrote about this, like everything else, on my blog. This had the unexpected side effect of serving as a classifieds ad for someone to replace him as my travel buddy.

The first person who wrote me was very excited about how we could party all over the world together. He loved alcohol and clubbing, two things I hate. The contrast made me realize how lucky I had been to be traveling with someone like Todd.

The next person who suggested traveling with me was a guy named Carl. He was a nondrinking internet marketer who liked eating healthy food. Just by comparison he seemed great. Even though I wasn't looking for a replacement, I figured I may as well invite him along to travel with me for a single trip.

I was about to leave on a cruise from the Dominican Republic to Spain. A single-person cabin cost the same as a double, so I gave him instructions on how to book it. He did so, and we agreed to meet in the Dominican Republic.

Two days before he arrived in Santo Domingo, I took a weekend trip across the island to Haiti. I had a great time there and was a bit cocky when I returned, as I had just gone through the ghettos of the poorest country in the hemisphere and hadn't been mugged or attacked.

Pleased with my newly confirmed invincibility, I opted to take a shortcut to dinner which would save me one minute. Rather than take the wide well-lit boulevard, I took the dark alley that bordered a crumbling concrete building and a cemetery. I got mugged, and they took my passport.

Replacement passports happen quickly, but not instantly. Carl arrived the night before the cruise, and I still didn't have a passport. He'd be beginning, and possibly finishing, the journey alone.

He booked a room in the same hotel, but came up to mine to meet. I told him about my passport predicament, and he told me about a conspiracy theory he believed. It involved the moon landing. I rather politely expressed my disinterest in the topic and he replied by describing another conspiracy theory he believed. This one involved aliens.

With each story I heard, I became slightly less polite. Two hours later, still talking about conspiracy theories, I was telling him bluntly to shut up and go to sleep. By this point we were talking about the lizard people. Or he was, anyway.

Suddenly losing my passport seemed like a blessing in disguise. I wasn't particularly eager to be stuck on a ship with a guy whose only interest was to share conspiracy theories I didn't care about. How had he failed to mention this in his email?

I got my passport the next day, after the ship had already sailed. The following day I flew to Puerto Rico, then to Anguilla. I slept on the lawn of the airport and was surprised how freezing it was at night in such a tropical place. I woke up, walked seven miles to the ferry terminal, only to realize that I was $5 short in fare. Out of options and nearly out of time, I then hitched a ride to an ATM with a guy I was sure was going to rob me. He didn't, so I made the ferry to Saint Maarten. From there I took a city bus to the other side of the island and walked to the ship. I arrived at lunch right as he was explaining the story to random people at his table. They probably thought it was a set-up.

The conspiracy theory talk was mostly over after a day or so. It was like it was all pressurized into his brain and just had to come out. He turned out to be one of the most earnest people I've ever known, very smart, and perpetually cheerful. Even when he and I are arguing and calling each other idiots, we're always both laughing.

–

A few years later, we went on a second cruise together. I'd gotten a few friends together to do a cruise that went from Florida to London, and one needed a roommate just as Carl decided that he wanted to go.

"Look, I have a roommate for you. He can be pretty weird, but he's a really good guy."

So Carl and Ben became roommates. They were about as different as people can be, but I had hoped that they would like each other anyway. And they did, mostly.

Carl never talked about conspiracy theories anymore, but instead had become obsessed with bizarre diets with dubious health claims. I had visited him in Shanghai and he was eating butter, bitter Chinese greens, and nearly-raw steak. No seasoning, nothing else.

As he embarked he told me about his newest diet, the 80/10/10 diet, which apparently meant that he ate nothing but bananas. Preferably nearly rotten bananas. He didn't tell Ben about the diet.

Two days later, Ben pulled me aside.

"Hey, I don't want to alarm you, but our entire room is full of bananas. Literally, every drawer and cupboard is full of rotting bananas."

He thought that Carl was crazy, an idea that has crossed all of our minds at least once. I explained the diet, which may not have done much to convince him that he wasn't crazy.

The cruise was fifteen days long, but Carl was panicked by day six. He had eaten all of the bananas on the ship. There were over a thousand passengers, and originally enough bananas for all of them, but Carl had eaten the entire stock by himself. Eating on cruise ships always becomes just a little bit competitive with my friends, but that's an achievement that none of us will ever hope to match. He reluctantly switched to honeydew melon, but didn't ever exhaust the supply.

On the next cruise, Carl's obsession was finance. Specifically, he was absolutely certain that the US stock market was going to crash. He had put all of his money, plus all of the money he could get from credit cards, on a stock that was triple-leveraged against the market. If the market went down a dollar, Carl would make something like ten dollars. But if it went up?

He explained his certainty to many skeptical and uninterested passengers at lunch. They thought he was crazy, too, so I dared not tell them the banana story. He had become a bit more grounded, though. He argued that even if he was wrong, he was young enough to rebuild. And if he was right, he'd be rich. I didn't hate that logic.

The market went up significantly. His losses piled up until he had no choice but to sell at a massive loss, bankrupting himself. The market still hasn't gone down. He now works on a cruise ship as an art auctioneer, which he does very well at and loves.

Ulrich - Panama City
Written in Marmaris, Turkey

My girlfriend at the time subscribed to a newsletter called the Caretaker Gazette. In it were short classifieds from landowners looking for nomads to take care of their property while they were away in return for a place to stay. It was fascinating reading. The offers ranged from farms which required experience with oxen to remote cabins.

One day she forwarded me an ad from a guy who had a private island in Panama, where I happened to be at the time. He was looking for someone to watch over it for a month or two. I wasn't going to be there that long, and was in fact about to leave, but I've always had a fascination with private islands. Even if I weren't going to visit his, I ought to at least meet him.

We met at a café called La Novena in Panama City. It was a vegan restaurant run by a man who absolutely loved Beethoven. The restaurant was named after his ninth symphony, and all of the decorations were Beethoven themed. He was an ex-engineer, and it showed. I always liked watching him carefully monitor exactly how many salt flakes were added to a dish.

Ulrich was immediately likable. He was warm and friendly, and had a smile that made him look younger than the thirty-something years old he was. We talked about the island a bit and then about ourselves. We bonded over our mutual love of Panama and travel in general.

It came up in conversation that I had previously been well known in the pickup community, having lived and taught alongside the best pickup artists in the world in Hollywood, California. Like most guys, he was fascinated with the topic. How did girls react when I told them, he asked?

I told him about my recent trip to Hong Kong. There I had stayed with a couple who, on my last night, had hosted a small barbecue on Lamma island off the coast of Hong Kong. The couple thought that pickup was the most interesting thing ever, so they told a friend they had invited about my involvement in it. She was repulsed and horrified.

Most girls take it well, I told him, but the least

secure tend to be offended by it, believing that it must be manipulative, and that they would be easily manipulated. The girl listening oozed with insecurity.

He laughed and said that it sounded like his ex-girlfriend, Jane.

It turns out it was his ex-girlfriend Jane, who was traveling through Hong Kong. It was absolutely astonishing to me that he was able to identify his ex-girlfriend simply by a display of her insecurity.

Five years later I had moved to San Francisco and was attending a book launch party for a close friend named Olivia who wrote a book called The Charisma Myth. I walked into the ballroom and heard someone call my name. I looked in the direction from which the call came but didn't see anyone I recognized.

Finally my eyes fixed on someone I hadn't seen in a long time. It turns out Ulrich was also friends with Olivia. How improbable was it that I would meet his girlfriend in Hong Kong, then him in Panama, and then run into him randomly again in San Francisco many years later?

We spent a little while catching up. He finally settled down in San Francisco aboard an Icelandic car ferry that he had parked downtown on one of the piers. That seemed like the right home for someone like him.

John – Qatar
Written in the Mediterranean Sea

Todd and I were wholly unprepared for Qatar. It was a two-day layover that didn't cost us any more than a one-hour layover, and such a short stop didn't warrant much planning. In fact, we hadn't planned at all. Todd bought his entry visa at the airport, but my credit card wouldn't work there. Upon further inspection, I realized that it had just expired the previous day. Todd paid for my visa, too.

We hopped into a cab and asked for the city center. The cab driver was confused.

"City center? Are you sure?"

Not knowing anything about Doha, Qatar, we figured going to the center of the city was the logical choice. We'd get there, walk around, see the city, and then find our way to a hostel that we had booked online. The driver shrugged and drove us to the city center. We got out to a yellow sandstorm haze, through which we could barely see the many glass skyscrapers.

Something felt strange. We walked a block and realized that not only was every business closed, they had never been opened. The entire downtown was being built all at once, and the only people in the city were the construction workers. That's why the driver was so confused-- we asked to be dropped off in a city that didn't quite exist yet.

It took forever to get another taxi. Even if the center of downtown wasn't a ghost town, there was another problem. The old taxis had recently been taken off the road, but there weren't enough new ones to keep up with demand. All over town it took fifteen to thirty minutes to get a cab to stop for you.

We finally made it to our hostel. It was impeccably clean, bright, and airy. The main living room had pillowed nooks against the walls and a big rug and pillow sitting area in the center. It was my first time in the Middle East, and it was everything I expected it would be.

The hostel was nearly empty. Qatar is a tiny country that protrudes from Saudi Arabia into the Persian Gulf. There's a US military base there, but not much tourism. As far as we could tell, the only guests at the hostel were us and John, a sixty-year-old British guy who lived in Australia. We were given an eight-bed room to ourselves, and I'm sure John had the same.

In paying for the room, we discovered that we had a small crisis on our hands. My credit card had expired, and I had recently lost my debit card. Todd only had one debit card, but he had accidentally paid his credit card bill from the wrong account and had overdrafted it. He had one credit card, but no one accepted credit cards there. Only ATMs and cash, and we had no working ATM card and almost no cash.

We emailed and got family members to Western Union us some cash while Todd straightened out his banking situation, but the money wouldn't arrive until right before we left. For dinner we paid a dollar for a big bag of pita bread, which we shared.

The one thing we really wanted to do in Doha was to go out to the desert and ride 4x4s in the dunes. We counted our beans and decided that we just barely had enough to take a taxi to the desert, split one 4x4, and ride back. Better than nothing.

We left the hostel and were glad to see John returning from somewhere in a cab. We yelled at him to hold the cab for us so that we wouldn't have to wait. We exchanged pleasantries, and as an afterthought asked if he'd like to go ride 4x4s in the dunes with us.

"Sounds like fun. Let me change me clothes right quick!"

I would have laid odds one hundred to one

against him joining us, but I was glad he agreed. I realized I had to give more credit to seniors who would travel to the Middle East all by themselves and stay at a youth hostel.

The three of us piled into the taxi and headed to the dunes. We made small talk, and the topic of our recent insolvency came up. As we described our situation, I felt very much like a scammer must feel. We didn't mean to manipulate, but as we spoke truthfully I knew that there was almost no way he could avoid offering us money.

"Well, I could loan you boys some money. How much do you think you'll need?"

He gave us about a hundred dollars in Qatari Riyal, which alleviated all of our concerns.

We learned that he had a grown up son in England, but no wife. He lived in Australia for most of the time, but liked to travel around as well. Like us, he was offered a free stopover in Qatar and couldn't resist seeing what it was all about. He had that charming British dialect where he said "me" instead of "my". His mustache made him look like a British jungle explorer; I bet he looks more like himself with a Panama hat on than without.

There were two types of 4x4s available: red ones that didn't have all that much power and green ones with a lot of power. Wanting to economize and not seem frivolous with the loan, we chose the smaller ones. He chose the big one and suggested that we each take turns on it.

I remember a lot from that day: flying over the dunes into the air on the green 4x4, trying to go down an impossibly large drop and rolling over the little red 4x4, watching Qataris pull through the sand in Lexuses with gaudy Loius Vuitton logos plastered all over them.

But what I remember most was the smile on John's face after he did the big jump with the green 4x4. Huge smile plastered on his face, he looked at us and said something like, "Well isn't that fun, boys?"

The taxi ride out there had been more expensive than we had anticipated. If he didn't come with us, we wouldn't have had enough money to make it back. We were so grateful to him for loaning two strangers money so that we could enjoy our short trip in Qatar. We paid him back the day we left, but I like to also think that he made out pretty well on the deal, getting to have some thrills that most guys his age don't have.

Felicio - Las Vegas
Written in Crete

When my friends and I were in college, we bought a school bus. Not a short bus, but an enormous forty-foot long yellow beauty. We spent a summer tearing out its innards, replacing them with carpeting, cabinetry that we built, insulation, and couches that we bought on Craigslist. It was our Taj Mahal on wheels.

Our first road trip took us from Austin,Texas to Key West, Florida and back, and our second major trip took us up to Vancouver, Canada. Our third road trip was an easy one, just a trip to Las Vegas and back.

This was the age of dollar gallons of gas and

our gas tank held one-hundred gallons, which meant that we almost never stopped, not even to switch drivers. Despite the fifty-five mile an hour governor, we could make it to Las Vegas on just two tanks of gas and in just over a day.

I began to get nervous as we approached Deming, New Mexico. I'm the furthest a person can get from superstitious, so I believe that there must be some scientific reason why things always go wrong in Deming. The last time the bus came through the area, we blew out a tire. In times past I've lost a transmission and hit a bird which knocked off my side-view mirror.

We made it through Deming without incident. I was relieved and felt foolish for assuming something would go wrong once again.

Shortly after, our air brakes stopped working so well. The reserve of air needed to keep the brakes off was filling up much more slowly than usual, meaning that any time we went down a hill a buzzer would go off, indicating that if we used the brakes much more, they would eventually stay on involuntarily.

We drove cautiously all the way to Kingman, Arizona. The situation got worse and worse, so we decided to stop and check it out. The two most mechanically-inclined of our group decided that we needed a new belt, so they took some measurements and hitchhiked their way into Vegas. The guy giving them a ride showed them a huge knife and told them not to try anything funny. They didn't.

The rest of us left the bus on and played poker in the back. We had intended to build bunk beds in the back room but ran out of time, so we'd often sit in a circle and play poker back there.

At some point we worried that we were burning too much fuel, so we turned off the bus and waited with the lights off for our friends to return. They finally made it back with some belts and tools. We turned the key to turn the bus on again, but it wouldn't start. We tried again and again, but nothing happened. There was power, but the engine wouldn't turn over.

It was dark and we were parked in the breakdown lane of a major highway. The bus shook with every car that whizzed by. We held up another sign asking for help, not knowing exactly what it was we needed. Cars continued to speed by.

Finally a man named Felicio and his son stopped. He popped the hood and looked around with his flashlight. While he diagnosed the problem with the friends who understood engines, I talked to his son. Out of nowhere he said,

"You should see my dad drive through the desert with the lights off when the cops are chasing him."

I left that one alone. Was he making this up?

Was his dad a coyote or a drug dealer or something? He seemed so nice and friendly.

Felicio finally decided that he had done all he could for the night. He promised to come back the next morning at seven. We all fell asleep to the swaying of the bus as the cars drove by on their way to Las Vegas.

The next morning we were all up and ready at seven. No sign of Felicio. Eight came and there was still no sign. Finally around eight thirty, Felicio arrived in his truck. He brought his friend, a bunch of tools, and a spare battery.

His friend got to work, and he suggested that he drive all but a couple of us to Las Vegas for the day. He thought repairs might take a while, and he was concerned that everyone would be bored. We tried to refuse his kindness, but he insisted. So two of us stayed with his friend and the bus while he drove the rest to Vegas.

By the time he returned his friend had decided that the starter needed to be replaced. He removed our starter and we headed into the city with it. He first took us through junk yards and to his friends houses, trying to find a suitable replacement on the cheap, but we had no luck.

Eventually we went to an auto store and ordered the new starter, which wouldn't come for two days. For the next couple days he came by in the morning to drive us to Vegas, brought us back at night, and worked on the bus whenever there was something to do. We constantly tried to give him money or pay for his gas, but he refused it all. He once begrudgingly allowed us to buy him lunch at a fast food chicken joint called El Pollo Loco.

The new starter came, he and his friend installed it, but the bus still didn't work. People's schedules were beginning to be stretched, and we needed to make an executive decision soon. Either we pay a lot of money to a mobile mechanic and hopefully have the bus fixed at some unknown price, or we abandon it.

A sheriff came by one day and put a sticker on the bus. If it wasn't moved within twenty-four hours, it would be towed. There would be no penalty to us, but if we wanted to get it back we would have to pay $500. After a lot of deliberation, we decided to leave the bus on the side of the road and abandon it.

We rented a car to drive back to Austin, loaded what we could into it, and said goodbye one last time to the bus. One friend put some flowers from the side of the road under the windshield wiper. All of us cried as we saw it fade in the rear view mirror. We had put so much time and money into that bus, and it had taken us on such great trips. It was a sad end to the chapter.

The next day, still driving back to Austin, we got a phone call from Felicio. We didn't have the heart to tell him that we were abandoning it, so we had just stopped calling him. I answered and he was jubilant.

"I saw that the bus was gone today! I'm so glad that you guys got it working! It was really nice to meet all of you! I hope your trip..."

"Actually, Felicio, it got towed. We gave up."

"Why did you do that? If you told me, I would have towed it myself and fixed it up for you."

Of course he would have. He was the nicest guy any of us had ever met. We had a conference and decided to all kick in the $500 to get the bus out of impound. We called Felicio and told him that it was his. Hopefully he could fix it and use it to take his family on trips. He insisted that he was going to fix it and give it back to us, but we told him to keep it. When we got home we mailed him the title.

I never spoke with Felicio again. In my mind he fixed the bus, loved it, and took his family on all sorts of great road trips around the country. I was scared to call him because I didn't want to risk shattering the fantasy. By the time I decided to call him I couldn't find his number. We got our money's worth out of the bus, and it went to a better home when we were done. Maybe he and his family still use it.

Toby – Tokyo
Written in Aqaba, Jordan

The second time Todd and I visited Tokyo we weren't messing around: we booked a flight for a full two months. Oblivious when we booked to the fact that it was cherry blossom season, we suddenly found it difficult to find a place to stay. Everyone wants to be in Tokyo late March to early April for cherry blossom season.

We found a place for the first three weeks. It was a room in a mansion, which was very exciting to us until we came to understand that the word mansion just means apartment in Japanese. It was a good mansion, though. It had a fancy toilet with a heated seat, real wood-paneled walls, frosted sliding windows, and a good-sized bedroom. Best of all, it was just a couple minutes away from Shibuya station, my favorite area in Tokyo.

In Panama we had no problem finding a place to work out. We were committed to never missing a workout on our trip, and we were lucky to find a gym directly next to our apartment building. Best of all, admission was just one dollar per day.

Tokyo was different, though. I don't know for sure, but I'd wager that you need to show a Japanese passport to get a membership. That's just how things are over there. Besides, we were doing a Crossfit program, which meant that even a normal gym doesn't always have the proper equipment.

We sat in our mansion and tried to look up online places we could work out. Prospects seemed bleak so we eventually gave up.

About an hour later, the door opened. In bounded a guy who looked our age, but was actually seven years older, with spiked red hair and a huge infectious smile. In one hand he held a small suitcase and in the other he held a kettlebell.

Todd and I looked at each other, bewildered. And then we looked at Toby, who was surprised to be stared at in disbelief.

"Well, hey there fellows..."

Within an hour we were doing a Crossfit workout. Swings, snatches, weird push-ups with our feet on the table. We became fast friends.

Toby was a lawyer from London who decided he didn't like law so much. So he quit his firm and became an acupuncturist. He's the kind of acupuncturist who responds to every skepticism with good humor and humility ("Who knows, maybe it is placebo! Just as long as it helps people!"), yet learns how to read Chinese characters so that he can read original sources.

When he first moved to Tokyo a year or so before, he refused to speak any English at all, so he was one of very few foreigners I knew there who had many Japanese friends.

Toby, like myself, liked finding abandoned buildings. He once found a row of five mansions (by the English definition, not Japanese), that were completely abandoned. We climbed the wall to the pool, fell into the bushes, and then explored all of the houses. And, of course, we took our shoes off before entering, as we would do for any Japanese household.

During one visit he told me that he had found an abandoned temple in the mountains of Chiba. We should go there, he said, and camp out overnight. The idea sounded reasonable enough.

Toby, his girlfriend Satoko, and I met the next morning. I had the smallest backpack, allotting myself an aggressively small amount of water. Toby had a medium sized bag, and Satoko had a huge one. We all had food in our backpacks, but

Toby had the most. He'd brought tons of marinated meat for a barbecue.

We took jabs at Satoko for her huge bag, which left her unruffled. She'd been hiking and camping for many years with her father, she said. She knew what to pack.

Once in a while Satoko would fall behind. At first I thought that she was tired, but then I realized that she was going into the woods and shrubs to find banana peels that we were throwing to the side. When we asked, she said that they don't decompose quickly.

I started running out of water very quickly. Halfway up the mountain, which was much taller than I had expected, I was rationing. One sip, then I'd wait another fifteen minutes. I was determined not to die of dehydration and, more importantly, not appear as though I hadn't packed enough water.

The temple was incredible. It was abandoned, but not decrepit. Toby found a straw mat inside and rolled it out over the floorboards so that we could put our sleeping bags on it. He opened the rice-paper doors on the front and revealed a sweeping view of sunset over the mountains of Chiba mountains.

Then he built a fire in a rocky alcove and began barbecuing all the meat. But before we could eat, Satoko put some small towels into a pot, filled it with her water, and gave us each a warm towel with which to wash our face and hands.

The meal was a feast. Despite building an enormous appetite from all of the climbing, we couldn't finish all of the meat. When we were done, Satoko used more of her water to make us all herbal tea. I think she knew that we were both extremely thirsty but that we wouldn't accept her water due to machismo. But who can refuse tea?

We slept with the windows open, listening to the cicadas.

The next morning we woke up to see an elderly Japanese couple looking into the temple. We composed ourselves and greeted them. They were amused that I could speak some Japanese and in awe of Toby's mastery of the language. They offered us every single beverage they had brought with them, and would not possibly allow us to decline. We offered them some walnuts, which they politely ate one or two of.

Toby told them about our hike, and said that we were going to go to an onsen, a Japanese bathhouse, afterwards. They asked if we wanted a ride, but we told them we were going to hang out for an hour before descending and didn't want to slow them down. They said that it would be no problem. We insisted that it was far too much of an imposition, and they eventually continued their hike down the other side of the mountain.

An hour later we followed, walking through the

stunning pine forest. We saw a snake slither across the path and plenty of huge spiders in webs. Satoko promised that they weren't poisonous.

When we got down, we were greeted by the elderly couple. Not only had they waited for us, but they had also made some phone calls to determine the best bathhouse for us. They took us there, and then snatched our trash from Satoko's hands, insisting that they would sort it as was required in Japan at the time, and dispose of it for us.

It is impossible to compete with Japanese hospitality, especially in rural Japan.

The onsen was indeed excellent. The water rose from deep below the earth through a layer of compacted leaves, so that it came out thick and nearly black. Something about this made it beneficial for you. It was a perfect end to another Japanese adventure, and just one of many I'd have with Toby over the years.

Ayumi – Fujieda, Japan
Written in the Red Sea

If you're going to Japan, he said, you've got to meet up with Ayumi. My friend Jesse, owner of the Samovar Tea Lounges in San Francisco, and I were talking about my upcoming trip to Japan. Ayumi and her family were tea growers in the Shizuoka region of Japan, an area known for exceptional green tea.

I emailed Ayumi and she invited me to come visit them. The invitation was warm, but vague. I couldn't tell if I was invited to stay for the night or just for the day. I planned my train to arrive early enough to spend just the afternoon, but left my next day empty.

When I arrived at Fujieda station, Ayumi was waiting for me in a narrow pickup truck. We exchanged greetings in English and Japanese and began driving to the tea farm.

"How long will you stay?" she asked.

"Oh, well... my schedule is pretty flexible. I could leave tonight or tomorrow morning, whichever is more convenient for you."

She frowned.

"Only one day? You should stay for a week or two at least."

I thought that was some gesture, inviting a complete stranger to live with you for a couple weeks.

The scenery along the drive became rural quickly. Small houses stood in front of bamboo groves. More often than not their front yards were rice paddies. It was persimmon season, and many of the houses had persimmon trees. I couldn't help but think about how different life must be as a farmer in rural Japan.

We arrived at the tea farm at last. It occupied the better part of the hill, perfect rows of tea bushes, all of them trimmed perfectly except for one. Two workers were standing with the trimmer, waiting for me. I held one end of it, a worker held the other, and we walked along the row trimming the bush and collecting the leaves. It was the spring harvest, and they had saved one row just so that I could see what it was like to collect tea.

From there we hauled the bags of tea to a tea processing factory. The air was so thick with the scent of steamed green tea that breathing felt like drinking it. Machines clunked and whirred to shape the tea, steam it, and move it around the factory. Ayumi's family was part of a collective of organic tea growers who all used this factory. We dumped huge bags of tea leaves into the hopper at the front, and she collected some processed tea in the back for me to bring home.

From the tea factory we went to their home. The best way I could describe the house would be to call it a tribute to wood. A central column rose from the floor to the ceiling of the second floor-- it was a varnished tree trunk with the bark removed and branches cut short. Beautiful hand-carved wooden screens rested above the rice paper screens that divided the rooms. The dining room table looked to be a cross-section of an enormous redwood tree.

We sat down for a meal. Her family was there-- her father, mother, and sister– and they told me their story.

Her father was one of the pioneers of organic tea farming in Japan. He started farming organically back in the seventies when no one really appreciated it. Knowledge was hard to come by back then, so the tea came out bad at first, and every lesson was hard-won. Eventually other families began farming organically, so progress sped up a little bit.

Ayumi was one of few second-generation farmers out there. Everyone else wanted to go to the city, she said. It was a point of genuine sadness for her, possibly because her peers were leaving, possibly because it was a peril to the tea industry.

Everything in the meal was made from scratch. Ahh, yes, we caught this mackerel earlier today. These bamboo shoots are from the backyard. This miso soup comes from soybeans we grew and fermented for months in that box over there. Everything was incredible, but they gave the impression that it was just a normal meal for them.

The next day we finally had tea. Her father made me a sencha using an incredible amount of leaves and not very much water. It was strong and delicious, the best sencha I've had to date. He spoke no English, and my Japanese leaves a lot to be desired, so mostly we just enjoyed the tea together.

After tea we went back out to the tea farm to weed. I wanted to help, but I was wearing sandals and they were concerned about snakes. So I sat there on the side and watched all of them, even the eighty year old patriarch, work their fields as they'd been working them for forty years.

Ayumi and her family are an anomaly in the tea world. I know this because nearly every serious tea person I've met not only knows Ayumi, but has stayed at her tea farm. They're liberal with their invitations, and so warm that everyone always returns.

Five years later I sat drinking tea in Las Vegas in a house that was serving double-duty as headquarters for a tea business. We drank tea at their table and I looked at the huge photos of tea farms that hung on the wall. One looked very familiar.

"This next tea is a green tea from a family in Fujieda…"

Clement - France
Written in the Red Sea between Eritrea and Yemen

Todd and I arrived in France. He had spent time there before and had a lot of ideas for things for us to do, but there was one sight that we both wanted to see for the first time: the Catacombs of Paris. The Catacombs are a series of tunnels underneath Paris. They have a storied past, but are best known for the caches of human bones that rest within them. During the 1700s, bodies were dumped into the Catacombs because there was no where else to put them.

A quick search brought us the bad news that only a tiny portion of the catacombs were available to visitors. Just half a kilometer was covered in glass, and a small entrance fee would allow one to look through the glass and see some bones. Underwhelming, to say the least.

A more thorough search revealed that there was a subculture within Paris of "Cataphiles", people who found ways into the catacombs and tried to stay one step ahead of the "Cataflics", the special Catacomb police. The Cataflics constantly blocked entrances found or created by the Cataphiles, and patrolled the catacombs to keep them out.

We found a gallery of photos from the catacombs, tracked down the guy who took them, and emailed him. Would he be willing to take a couple of travelers from the United States into the catacombs?

"Yes we can take you into the catacombs!" came the reply. Just bring some rubber boots.

We met Clement on the outskirts of Paris. He was friendly, cheerful, and clearly an expert on the Catacombs. We thought we were meeting up with some random punk who had worked his way in, but Clement was about as close to a Catacomb historian as one could be.

As we walked to the entrance, Clement told us of the history of the Catacombs. Paris' underground was originally a stone quarry. When it started becoming built up, buildings would sometimes sink into the ground because the quarry was below it. To combat this problem they built a tunnel system that mirrored the Paris streets. They could then follow the streets underground, see what was there, and support it if necessary.

But that's just the beginning. Over the years the catacombs were used for water storage, smuggling, partying, war bunkers, and just about anything else you could imagine using a massive network of tunnels for. We were entranced by his French-accented description.

The entrance was down a long tubular brick tunnel which, we were assured, was no longer used by trains. Beyond where the sunlight reached there was a small hole chipped out of the brick wall. Clement lowered himself through it into the catacombs and we followed.

We were immediately knee deep in cold spring water. Along the tunnel ran thick braids of copper cable, France's first telephone system. We followed the cables deeper into the tunnels.

Over the course of four or five hours we saw everything we hoped for and a whole lot more. We saw German trenches that still had communications and lighting equipment in them. "Achtung!" was stenciled on the walls with a sentence that essentially warned soldiers that the French were on the other side of the wall. We saw a huge cavern, still strewn with detritus, that was used for an infamous party in the seventies. There was a cistern below a church, an underground library, and a peek through a crack into a still-functioning building.

And then, finally, we reached the bones. At first you'd see an odd femur on the ground and you'd gingerly step over it, because human bones are a little bit gross. Soon after the density of the bones multiplied and you had no choice but to step on them. Beyond that the ceiling fell and you were forced to crawl, military style, across the bones and mud.

We ended up in a small circular room. It was the bottom of a well where bodies had been thrown. A look up the shaft revealed arms and legs sticking out of the walls. All around us were miscellaneous pieces of bone, vertebrae, fingers, chips of scapula or sternum.

That's when I realized that had always wanted some human bones. This was my one chance to get them, and I couldn't squander it. From the mud I pulled up two chunks of skull and a single vertebrae. I put them in a plastic bag in my backpack and we continued on our way. I was surprised that no one else had any desire to bring back human bones.

Clement's plan was to exit through a manhole in downtown Paris. He climbed up the shaft on rusted metal rungs and tried to push the cover off the hole. It wouldn't budge. He came down and frowned.

"They've put bricks on it, probably. They're always trying to get one step ahead of us."

So we instead retraced our path to the old train tunnel. Right as we reached the thick telephone cables, a man pushed past us. Eager to practice my French I gave him a bonjour, which he didn't reciprocate.

"Don't talk to them. Thats' the police. They are surrounding us."

We were caught. With the single officer behind us and several waiting for us at the entrance, we had no way to escape. We were lined up single file in the pitch black tunnel. The only source of illumination was the headlamps of the police, and they used them to search us, one by one.

I was last, and all I could think about was the bones. There must be serious consequences for taking bones out of the catacombs. I kept trying to think of some sort of plan or excuse, some way to get out of being caught, but I couldn't come up with anything.

For a brief moment none of the lights were on me. I could easily open up my backpack and throw the bones behind me. They'd blend in with the rocks and I'd never be caught. I began the motion but stopped myself. This was my only chance to get human bones, and they were special-- they were from the Catacombs. Surely I would come up with a plan.

It was my turn, and I had come up with no plan. I slowly unzipped my backpack, waiting for the inevitable reveal of the loot. Through the crack of the half-opened zipper I saw the bones and I saw a baseball cap. In one motion I stuffed the bones into the cap and pulled it out of the bag.

"This is my hat..."

I went for the next item, and wasn't questioned. Then another, and another. They rifled through the half-empty bag and let me put my things back in. The bones went undetected.

Of course, we were still in trouble. The marched us out of the tunnel towards the police van that was waiting on the road. Clement explained what was going on.

"They want to give us a fine, but they know that you will not pay it because you are not French. They are deciding whether to bring us to jail or not."

In the front I heard Todd, chipper as ever, chatting with the police. I knew just enough French to understand the gist of what he was saying.

"Oh, we just love France and your history. We know we shouldn't have been there, but it is so historic. Such an interesting country..."

I began to become nervous again. Surely they would itemize everything in my bag if they took us to jail. I considered ditching the bones again, but couldn't bring myself to do it. If I was going to go to jail and get caught with the bones, so be it.

For an hour we sat on the sidewalk while they decided our fate. It seemed that the tides swung both ways, one officer really wanting to bring us there, but the one that Todd had chatted with pushing to let us go. Finally, we were released.

Clement got a ticket, but refused to let us pay for it. He kept insisting that he wasn't really going to pay it anyway, but I had a hard time believing that. I had earrings made out of the bones, but lost one in a cruise ship karaoke contest gone bad.

Thomas – Egypt
Written in The Aden Gulf

From the airport in Amman, Jordan I texted my friend. We had both capitalized on an error fare that brought us on the same route, separated by a few weeks, for just a couple hundred bucks. Our next stop was Cairo, so I asked him if he had any tips. Oh yes, he said, you have to call Thomas.

He explained that Thomas had a hostel right next to the pyramids. You could see them from the roof. Besides running his hostel, he also gave the most amazing tours. He mentioned that Thomas must be independently wealthy because it seemed as though he charged far less than it should cost.

I texted Thomas from the airport and asked if

he had rooms. No problem, he said. He asked what airport we were coming from, and when I replied he asked if we'd bring him two bottles of 10 Euro wine. Sure, no problem.

So the three of us, Todd, his girlfriend Shammy, and I, flew to Egypt, took a taxi, and arrived in front of Thomas' building. Outside one of his friends, or associates, offered us tea. We tried to decline, wary that we'd be charged dearly for it as sometimes happens in northern Africa, but he insisted. He never charged us anything.

Thomas texted us saying that he was running a little late, and could we meet him in front of the Pizza Hut? He would be the Egyptian guy with "two hot chicks", a phrase which was immediately off-putting. But we showed up anyway and met him and the two Dutch girls he was guiding around and hitting on gratuitously. They seemed really into it.

The six of us went to an Egyptian restaurant and ate a typical dish that involved lentils, spaghetti, and just about everything else. It was good. We went to pay, but he beat us there and paid for everyone. Normally this would be a friendly gesture, but I wondered if we were racking up a tab that would need to be settled in the end. We went to the fresh juice place next door, ordered, and he paid again.

It's around this time that I became nervous. We hadn't settled on any price for the rooms and I had no idea what he was paying for these meals. What figure would he quote us at the end, and how could we contest it? Thinking more about it, I had no idea whether my friend was well-traveled or not. Maybe he had fallen for a scam and baited us directly into it.

Todd, Shammy, and I exchanged concerned glances. We have all traveled a lot and know the signs.

We got back and saw our rooms, which were nicer than expected, and basked in the view from the roof. It offered a panoramic view of the pyramids, exactly like a postcard but in 3D and a lot wider. With the pyramids in full view, we discussed a tour with Thomas.

"What is your budget for the tour?"

"Well, how much does it cost?"

"Not that much. Just tell me how much you want to spend and I will make the tour for you."

"Well, we'd like to see the great pyramid, the ruins, the Sphinx, and anything else you think might be good."

"Okay, I think that will be about $30 each."

That seemed very reasonable to me, although I had no context for it. Either way, if we were being ripped off for some part of thirty dollars, I still felt like we were coming out of the situation in good footing. We agreed.

"I think it would be better if you gave me your

money so that I can pay people for you."

I hated the idea, but he was being so friendly that to disagree would be to disrupt rapport. No problem, I said. We each ponied up thirty dollars in Egyptian pounds and went to sleep.

The next morning we woke early in the morning and walked to a nearby restaurant to buy sandwiches. I asked for six ingredients, hummus, salad, falafel, vegetables, baba ghanoush, and beans. My friends copied my order. Instead of one sandwich with all of these ingredients, we were each handed six different sandwiches, each featuring one ingredient. We reached to pay, but again Thomas beat us to it.

Things got interesting at the gates to the pyramids. It appeared that we were there before opening hours, but Thomas pushed his way to the front of the line and started yelling. They yelled back, he exchanged some unknown quantity of money, and we were allowed in. We were the only ones there.

We walked the deceptively long path to the great pyramid, the biggest one. A similar scene ensued there, with Thomas arguing loudly with the guards. They yelled back and forth and right when it seemed we'd be kicked out, the guards accepted some other bundle of money and welcomed us warmly. It was a complete one-eighty.

The four of us had the pyramid entirely to ourselves, which is really quite amazing. We climbed up the stairs into the very center of the pyramid where the tomb lays. Thomas unplugged the ventilation machine so that it was dead silent. We all chose a place to sit and sat in silence, absorbing the magnificence of the chamber. Halfway through I got up and lay in the tomb, trying to imagine that I was a dead pharaoh and that the entrance was still closed.

The rest of the day was similar, but there was no more arguing. Everyone else seemed to love Thomas and would happily do whatever he wanted for a mysterious wad of cash. One guard turned a blind eye while we climbed a pyramid. Another let us in a tomb that wasn't meant for public access which featured original hieroglyphics that still had their original paint. It was truly spectacular. Someone made us tea. A kid spent a crazy amount of time taking all sorts of novelty photos for us, using different angles to make it look like we were stomping on the pyramids or touching the top with our fingers.

At a certain point, maybe halfway through, I realized that we were getting an excellent value for our thirty dollars. I have no idea how much of that was spent by Thomas and how much was pocketed, but it certainly seemed like we were getting the better end of the deal. He knew everything about the pyramids and the sphinx and was an excellent tour guide.

That night he ordered a huge meal delivered to the hostel. We had fish as well as hummus and the usual Middle Eastern accoutrement. As usual, he paid.

I was conflicted. He seemed like he was our friend and was very generous, but we still hadn't discussed his fee for the tour or the cost of our two rooms in the hostel. We were to leave the next morning. I brought up the idea that we should settle our bill, and he said that he would wake up early in the morning to make sure we got our taxi and that we could do it again. The cynical side of me worried that he wanted to limit our negotiation time.

We woke up the next morning, exhausted. He was there, also sleepy, waiting for us in the living room. We thanked him profusely for such a great experience, and were sincere. Egypt had exceeded all expectations and it was entirely due to him. We asked what we owed him.

"You brought me those two bottles of wine. I think we're pretty much even."

I couldn't believe it. For the first time ever in the Middle East, I argued to pay more. Surely we must owe him more for all of those meals and two nights at his hostel. He refused and said that if we felt that way we could pay it forward to other travelers, and that he was happy to have had us there.

Elliot – Tokyo
Written in Salalah, Oman

Todd and I booked our first place in Tokyo for three weeks. It wasn't available for the remaining five, but we figured that we'd have no problem finding a new place with so much time to do it. Soon that three weeks was two, and then one, and then we forgot we needed to look for another place until Todd realized we had just two days left.

We scrambled to find a new place to sleep in between bouts of karaoke and sushi binges, but nothing was available. It turns out we weren't the only ones that thought cherry blossom season may be a decent time in which to visit Tokyo.

At the time we kept a blog of modest popularity, with 1000 readers. At the end of one of the posts we wrote, "By the way, if you happen to have a large house in Tokyo, preferably in Shibuya, and have an extra couple beds that we can stay in for free, let us know."

It was tongue in cheek, but we thought that maybe someone might know someone who could rent us some space.

With just one day left, we received an email.

"A friend who reads your blog sent me your most recent post. As it happens, I do have a rather large place in Shibuya with two extra beds. I'd be happy to have you stay a week or so while you find somewhere else."

I think The Secret is complete nonsense, but...

We met Elliot at a vegan café in Shibuya called Crayon Cafe. We chose it because we were vegans at the time and Elliot didn't protest. We had assumed that he would be extremely weird. I mean, who in their right mind opens their home to two strangers and doesn't want anything in return? He was equally tentative about us, so the whole dinner was an exercise in feeling each other out and discovering that no one at the table was a psychopath.

We moved into his apartment the next day. It was in an embassy that he worked for, so his house was much larger than one would expect from Japan. It had two bedrooms and a small study that doubled as a third bedroom.

Over the next week, we became fast friends. We had similar senses of humor, were all nerds, and all loved Japan.

Todd and I were planning to go to the island of Yakushima the next weekend. All we really knew about it that it was a UNESCO World Heritage site, was about as far south as you can go in Japan unless you're in Okinawa, and that the forest was full of famous cedar trees. Yes, in Japan there are famous cedar trees.

Elliot's interest was piqued, so he bought train tickets and decided to join us. Our friend Brooke flew in from San Francisco, crashed on his couch, and made it a foursome.

I did the research on the internet. There were several trails that led to the peak and visited different cedar trees. One was argued to be the best, the Shiratani trail, so it was an easy choice. Japan is full of good signs, so I figured we'd just head down there, follow the signs, and have a nice multi-day hike. Along the trail were several mountain huts, free shelters that anyone could use. Easy.

Problems arose almost immediately. We arrived in Kagoshima, the closest port on the mainland, around five pm. We were then informed that the last ferry to Yakushima had just left, and that we could head up there the following day. We were given a tourist map of the city that looked like a placemat at a family-friendly restaurant chain.

We sat at an Italian restaurant in the station and pondered our next move. Hotels seemed to be scarce, and may be expensive. Way off in the middle of nowhere on our map was a single dot that said "cave". I joked that we should sleep in the cave and, for some bizarre reason, everyone agreed. I was then forced to take my own suggestion seriously.

We began walking towards the cave dot. Around halfway there, two things happened. First, the sky opened up and instantly drenched us. Second, we came across a giant cliff face. The cave was on the other side.

Sopping wet, we shuffled up the stairs. An hour after leaving the restaurant, we found the cave. It was a U-shaped cave in the side of a mountain, maybe one-hundred feet long in total. Wind whipped through one end and out the other, making it more of a wind-tunnel than a cave. Inside was a glass display case of some sort. It was freezing cold, but dry. We took off what layers we could and laid them out to try to dry them.

It's worth mentioning at this point that only Elliot had the foresight to bring any camping gear. He had a sleeping bag. None of us had anything else. The ground was cold, the wind chilled us, and none of us ever actually got dry. Brooke, determined to improve our situation, got up and went scouting. She found a bunch of cardboard boxes, neatly folded in Japanese fashion, and brought them in. At least they would provide some insulation.

We divided the boxes equally and made hard little beds.

"Does it smell like fish to anyone else in here?"

The boxes came from a sushi place, and were ostensibly the boxes in which the raw fish had arrived. Unwilling to give up our insulation, we added the fishy atmosphere to the list of injuries we attempted to endure to get a single night's sleep.

Of course, no one really slept. You'd drift off and then your body would wake up in the name of self-preservation and beg you to go somewhere warmer. But you'd stay in the fishy little cave and try to sleep for a few more minutes. To this day, sleeping on fish boxes in the cave has been my worst night of sleep.

As soon as the sun cracked over the horizon, we were all awake and ready to go. We folded the fish boxes back up and dragged ourselves out of the cave. We walked back down the cliff, all the way to the port, and boarded our ship.

The ship was a miracle. It was full of tatami mats upon which to sleep, but, more importantly, had a full Japanese bathhouse in it. This bathhouse included a sauna, which we quickly covered in its entirety with our wet clothes and bodies. By the time we arrived at Yakushima, we were rested, dry, and cheerful.

Yakushima is known for raining constantly, but we got a sunny day. We stopped at an outfitter to rent sleeping bags and walked along the small rural roads until we saw a sign that said

"Shiratani path". Shiratani was what we were looking for, so we entered the forest.

A few things were strange about the path, but Japan is always so strange that you sometimes fail to alarm when things seem off. First, we were the only people on the path. The sites I'd visited said that this was the most popular trail, so it seemed strange that we would have it to ourselves. Second, it wasn't actually a trail. There were pink ropes tied to trees, and we would just follow from one to the next. Sometimes there was a trail, but a lot of the time we just tromped through the woods from one rope to the next.

I finally began to become alarmed when we had been hiking for four hours and hadn't seen a single sign or waypoint. The whole hike was supposed to be four hours to the first mountain hut. Brooke had asked me if it was a difficult trail, I had told her no, but now she was climbing steep rocky hills using her hands and feet. She accused me of lying to trick her into coming.

Two hours later, it was dark. We could barely make out the ropes and still had no idea where we were. Every once in a while we'd imagine we saw a mountain hut, but it would just be a fallen tree or a bunch of bushes.

After eight hours we reached pavement. There was a small building that initially appeared to be a mountain hut, but turned out to be a bathroom. Next to it was a sign for the

Shiratani trail. It turns out the Shiratani path and Shiratani trail were two different things. We were now exactly where we were supposed to have started.

Exhausted, we climbed on top of the bathroom and unrolled our sleeping bags there. It was rough sleeping, but a massive improvement over the cave.

The rest of the trip went mostly without incident and was absolutely magnificent. We saw monkeys, deer, extremely old cedar trees, and incredible views.

One point of interest was our food. We brought very little, not wanting to lug much up the mountain. Besides fruits and nuts for snacks, we each brought one can of food to be our big dinner when we made it to the top. Each of us took a different tack.

Todd chose a can of coconut milk. It was fairly disgusting by itself, but had more calories than any other canned food.

I chose a can of garbanzo beans, for reasons I no longer remember. I ate the beans, and then when I admitted to myself that I hadn't brought nearly enough water, drank the bean water.

Elliot chose a can of Spaghetti-O's. If you don't know, these are the lowest quality pasta commercially available, drowned in thin red sauce.

"Dammit, I forgot to bring a fork!"

Searching for a solution, he came across a piece of styrofoam that had been protecting an apple he brought. Very slowly and methodically, he started pinching away little pieces of the styrofoam to fashion a fork. We made fun of him intensely, rubbing in his face the fact that we were already enjoying our bean water and coconut milk while he was wasting his time on a fork that would never work. Surely the little styrofoam tines would bend with the weight of even one Spaghetti-O.

But they didn't. His fork worked absolutely perfectly and he had the last laugh. I'm sure he doesn't think of that moment as his greatest triumph in life, but it's the one I remember most clearly. There's nothing better than succeeding when your friends are laughing at your inevitable failure.

Seven years later, we are still great friends. I stay with him every time I'm in Tokyo, and he was the one that figured out that islands in Canada were cheap enough to purchase. Of course, we ended up getting shipwrecked on our island and once again had to survive off not enough canned food.

Eve – Pacific Ocean
Written in Muscat, Oman

When I try to convince friends to go on cruises
with me, the objections stack up quickly. It's too
contrived, too expensive, and the other
passengers are too old. I can debate the first
two objections, but the last is hard to argue.
The average age of a cruise passenger is over
fifty, and on the long trans-oceanic cruises that
I prefer, the average age is probably a solid
decade beyond that.

The old people, though, are a highlight for me.
We are seated with them for every meal, and I
love the chance to get to know people I'd never
otherwise meet.

Ten friends and I were sailing across the
Pacific. A few of us broke off for lunch on the
second day and were seated at a table of eight.
At one point one of the couples began talking
about their daughter, who they said was about
my age.

The cruise happened at the tail end of me
taking a three-year break from dating. I wanted
to focus more on work, but had decided that I
would begin dating again on January first, just a
few months after the cruise.

"I'm happy to hear that you have a daughter,
because I am going to begin dating again in
January. Why don't we save me a lot of time and
set up an arranged marriage?"

I was, of course, joking. She hadn't really told me anything of substance about her daughter, nor had I seen a picture. She laughed, I kept kidding around, and by the time we left lunch, I was calling her "Mom" instead of Eve.

The cruise was seventeen days long. Mom and I bonded over our shared love of deals, and mild contempt for the outrageous prices of tour packages. She would come have tea with my friends and me once in a while, and we were once angrily shushed in the back of the theater while discussing our respective travel plans in Russia.

Every day she would show me a picture of her daughter, too distant to actually recognize her, or tell me something about her. She started sounding pretty interesting. I would tell her about myself and she would say, "This could be dangerous. She might actually like you."

Friendships on cruises are strange because they rarely last. The real world is too different from the world at sea and so not even the best intentions tend to result in emails being sent or phone calls being made. And this cruise was no different. We said our goodbyes and didn't bother to trade contact information.

Three months later I made a post to my blog announcing my triumphant return to the dating world. I asked my readers to introduce me to anyone with whom they thought I might be compatible. Submissions poured in, but I found the process of sifting through them more tedious than anything and found no great matches.

A couple weeks after the rest of the submissions, a straggler came in. A reader named Chloe, who I'd met previously at a local tea house, emailed saying that I should really meet her friend Jill. She copied both of us on the email. Discouraged from the other emails, I put off replying.

The next day I awoke to an email from Jill. She wrote a little bit about herself and asked my favorite flavor of ice cream. In the footer of her email was a link to her Instagram, which I clicked. I froze when I saw the first image in her feed.

I knew the people in it. It was my cruise Mom and her husband and I had just met their daughter.

I wrote Jill back immediately. Yes, I would love to go on a date, but more importantly, I know your mother and we need to play a prank on her. Realizing how crazy that sounded, I dug up a photo of us together and attached it.

We went on a date, it went well, and soon we were boyfriend and girlfriend. To preserve our ability to prank her mother, she never told her about us dating.

A few months in we booked a trip to Europe, and she thought that her parents should probably know where and with whom she was going. She told her mother she had a new boyfriend that she wanted her to meet. A date was set for a restaurant in Chinatown.

"Did my mother really like you?"

"Oh yes, we were really good friends on the cruise. We had tea together, lunch together, and we talked almost every day."

"But are you sure she actually liked you?"

"Of course. Why?"

"She's very critical of my boyfriends and never likes them. Maybe she was just being polite but didn't really like you."

The day came when I was to meet her mother, and I was nervous for the first time. We were about to ambush Eve, and with so much time and distance between our meeting, I could no longer be completely sure that she really did like me. Maybe this was about to be very awkward.

We walked into the restaurant and approached her.

"So nice to meet you," I said, and extended my hand.

"Nice to meet you, too," and then a pause...

"What did you say your name was, again?"

"Tynan."

"TYNAN?" Recognition flashed across her face and her eyes went wide. Her jaw dropped a little bit. Suddenly she put it into context and made sense of the situation.

"Oh, but you aren't REALLY dating!"

I put my arm around Jill and her jaw dropped again.

"Oh my god," she muttered, and turned completely around.

"I knew she didn't like you!" said Jill.

But Eve was just explaining the situation to her brother, who had also come for the great boyfriend meet-up. We were seated at a big table, and Jill asked her mother if she wouldn't prefer to sit next to her son.

The conversation at dinner was dominated by Eve and me. We talked about cruising, good deals, travel, and everything we had bonded over on the ship. She did like me, after all.

Amanda – Amsterdam
Written in Dubai

Some cities I love because they're full of things I like to do. Tokyo, Shanghai, and Budapest, for example. Others I love because of how they feel, but I don't always know what to do with myself there. Amsterdam is one of those cities. I love walking along the canals, I love seeing people biking, and I love the great art, but those things don't necessarily fill my days.

One morning my friends were going to the museums. Great choice, but I'd been to the Rijks and Van Gogh museums recently and wasn't particularly tempted to see the modern art museum. Most western European countries don't have much for tea, but I figured I'd take a shot in the dark and see if there was anywhere I could go sit and have some nice tea while writing or pondering my future.

One place stood out: Formocha. It wasn't clear whether it was actually a tea house or someplace that just sold tea, but regardless, it would be a nice one-mile walk along the canals.

The sun was out, which I noticed only because I hadn't seen it in weeks. I walked along the sunny side of the canals, enjoying seeing the drawbridges and houseboats. But when I arrived at Formocha, it was closed.

Through the big windows I could see a beautiful tea room, so I pressed my face against the glass and looked around a little bit. I'm a sucker for teaware and tea tables, so I figured I'd least take some inspiration after walking all the way there. Then I saw movement-- the owner, Amanda, was in the back.

I waved in apology, but she came to the door to say hello. I explained that I didn't realize she was closed and didn't want to bother her. I was only here for a day, but would come back next time I was in the city.

"You're already here. You should have some tea."

So she invited me in and asked what sort of tea I liked. I mentioned a few of my favorite oolongs, and she chose two from her collection and began to brew them in traditional Chinese tea ceremony style.

That's how I spent my morning: sitting in a

closed tea shop with Amanda, an extremely knowledgable and warm woman, talking about tea and travel and life. It occurred to me that there are some great experiences you can try to have, but that the best are often unexpected.

Both teas were fantastic, and so was the company and the view of the canals out the big storefront window. I learned about the history of tea, how it migrated from China to Japan, as well as the trends she noticed from her customers. They're mostly male, 30-50, and generally writers or artists or musicians. She used to have a tearoom where people could buy tea by the pot, but she switched to just selling loose tea so that she could be selective about who drank tea in the store. She only wants people who love tea; many people with no interest in tea or tea culture come because it's trendy.

As we got up to leave she asked which tea I liked better, and filled up a beautiful Formocha tin with it for me to take home. I wanted to pay, to express gratitude, but she was so warm and welcoming that I felt it would have been rude, like trying to pay my mother to cook me dinner. So I thanked her and promised to send a copy of my book, and to visit again next time I was in the city.

I walked past her old dog, the one whose eventual death will allow her to travel again, and back into the sunny streets of Amsterdam. I smiled, glad to have had the perfect morning in Amsterdam, and happy to now have someone to visit next time I'm there.

Lucia – Bucharest
Written off the coast of Djibouti

Convincing my friend Brian to go on a cruise with me had required a strong sales pitch. I told him of the wonderful days at sea, the interesting ports he would never otherwise see, the endless supply of seafood, beef, and lamb, and the fun seniors that you got to meet during dinner.

On that last point I was in danger of being called a liar. We sat at our table for our first dinner and the old couple, who just seemed like they must be Hungarian, preferred to scowl at us rather than converse. It may have been our youth, which does offend on occasion, or perhaps that we had ordered four entrees each. At our table of eight, four seats remained empty.

The next day the Magyars didn't show up. In their place sat a mid-sixties British couple, and in two previously vacant seats were two beautiful girls around our age.

Young people on cruise ships are extremely rare. I assume by default that my friends will be the only group with an average age below fifty, and am most often correct in my assumption. Questions like, "What made you decide to go on a cruise?" are phrased with bewilderment and slight suspicion. So you can imagine my surprise when two young passengers were seated next to us. I stared at Brian in astonishment.

I tried to engage the girls in conversation, but they were shy. They were from Romania, and English was a second, third, fourth, or maybe fifth language. They seemed to speak a lot of them. The one topic that brought them to life, though, was Romania. They were proud of their country and eager to tell us all sorts of stories about Bucharest and beyond.

The Hungarians never returned, so every night it was the six of us. The British woman, Barbara, would tell us stories of grievances she had against cruise lines, two of which were making their way through the courts. Her husband Andrew liked to describe complex flight routings through Europe ("Now, there's no international terminal in Brighton, so of course we took the motorway to London before flying to Lyon...") and past alcohol purchases at duty-free shops. Lucia, the older of the Romanian sisters, told us all about Romania, and her younger sister, Andreea, backed her up.

We became friends with the Romanian sisters and would often walk around the ship chatting with them after dinner. One night I proposed that we play a prank on the other two people at the table. The prank was meant to be good-natured fun for everyone, and I hoped that it might bring us closer together, as I had started to develop a bit of a crush on Lucia.

The plan I hatched was that Lucia and Andreea would show up to dinner early and ask the Brits to sit between them and us. They would then explain that we had scaled the exterior of the ship in the middle of the night, snuck into their room through the balcony, and slept on their floor. A running joke was the incredibly loud disco, whose music permeated our room, so we thought this extreme solution to not being able to sleep would be ridiculed.

But things didn't go according to plan.

Andreea was feeling seasick, so Lucia went alone to dinner. But before she reached the dining room, she ran into the Brits. She recounted our made-up story to them and they were aghast. We seemed like such good people, and in fact they had chosen to remain with us rather than transfer to the table of their friends, but now they realized that we were absolute monsters. Lucia must report us at once to security, they insisted.

She resisted reporting us, but they became more and more furious with us. They paraded her in front of a table of eight of their friends and told them the story. Lucia was getting deeper and deeper and didn't know what to do. The joke wasn't funny, but she didn't want to let us down or admit that it wasn't true.

Of course, we didn't know any of this when we sat down at the table. So we pretended to be oblivious to everyone's icy stares, acted like everything was normal, and tried to provoke reactions. Andrew coped with the awkwardness by doubling down on itinerary and duty-free stories, Barbara just glared at us.

The dinner was two hours of excruciating awkwardness. We wanted to back out of the story, but how? There was no way to coordinate and make sure everyone was on board, so we all endured the dinner without revealing the truth.

Brian and I left early to camp at the top of the stairs. Every day after dinner Barbara and Andrew took the elevator up to their room and the girls and we would walk up the stairs. I saw Lucia turning the corner, began to say something, and she widened her eyes to warn me. Behind her were Barbara and Andrew, escorting her to make sure I wasn't waiting for her. Which, of course, I was.

They passed me and I followed, since my room

was further down the hall. The British couple didn't realize I was following, so they talked about how horrible I was while I was two feet behind them. Only when they stopped at her door did they see me, ostensibly following. At that same time Brian returned from the bathroom and flanked them from the other side. They glared at both of us and entered the room silently.

Brian and I retreated to our own room. This was a catastrophe. The nice atmosphere at dinner was completely ruined because of us, the Brits hated us, Lucia was incredibly uncomfortable, and any overtures I would consider making towards her had just been made completely inappropriate.

Half an hour later Lucia came to our room. We all quickly agreed that the prank was a complete disaster and that something had to be done. But what? The options seemed to be to grit out the last six dinners in the face of awkward contempt, or to come clean and face the consequences. I thought about what I would want if I were in their shoes, and realized coming clean was the only option.

Everyone agreed, but Lucia was nervous. After all, she was the one who lied to them. We had put her in an incredibly tough position, so we agreed that we would make the apology ourselves and stress that it was entirely our idea.

The next day we criss-crossed the entire ship

looking for Barbara and Andrew. It took half an hour, but we finally spotted them in the café. We approached them, were greeted with a scowl, and began.

"There's something we need to tell you guys. We feel absolutely awful about this, but we didn't actually climb into the girls' room last night. It was a horrible prank gone wrong, and we feel absolutely terrible..."

Faces reddened. Barbara was the more furious of the two and kept repeating the phrase, "That is not on!"

We didn't know exactly what that Britishism meant, but we agreed with it, sure that she was right. We tried to stress that we had intended the prank to be fun and good natured and how sorry we were, but nothing we could say fixed the situation. Barbara began tearing up and stormed off. Andrew looked more disappointed than furious and quietly said that we should probably be gone before she got back, and that they'd be sitting elsewhere for dinner.

The mood at dinner that night was somber. The four of us sat alone, fielding accusatory looks from across the dining room. On the rare occasion a joke was cracked and any of us laughed, we could be sure that we were being watched and judged. We felt awful.

We sent a sincere letter of apology and chocolates to their room. One of them ran into Lucia and said that they would join us for dinner on the last day. We were forgiven, but we knew a lot of goodwill had been lost.

The final dinner was pleasant. No one mentioned the prank, and everyone just acted as though the previous five days had never existed. It was more peaceful reconciliation than outright jubilation, but we were thankful for it. We said our goodbyes and left the table in good spirits.

After dinner Brian, Lucia, Andreea, and I walked around the ship. We all loved cruising, even Andreea who had spent most of the trip in her cabin within sprinting distance of the toilet. This strange life away from land was coming to an end.

We paired off, me talking closely with Lucia, Brian and Andreea behind us. I felt the urge to kiss her, but thought that it might not be well received in front of her sister.

"Where did my sister go?"

It seems that Brian, who is gay and had only a platonic interest in Andreea, had sensed the atmosphere and did me the favor of giving us some privacy. I kissed her.

We spent the next hour or so talking and kissing on the deck, looking out over the ocean, but it was way past her bedtime. It was her first time in the US the next day and they had a tour planned for the early morning. I said goodnight and didn't even think to exchange email addresses with her, so preoccupied was I with the thought that I'd never see her again.

The next day I hoped we'd run into each other, but we didn't. I visited a friend in Florida and then headed to the airport. Thankful for free wifi, a luxury not found on cruise ships, I began to catch up on all of the sites I usually visited.

Many of these sites are travel deal sites, and there just happened to be a $400 flight to Bucharest that was available that moment. My flight was boarding and I had no way to contact Lucia, but her repeated description of Romania had me intrigued. I decided that the trip would be worth it whether I saw her or not. I booked the flight.

On my flight it occurred to me that this was the act of a really creepy guy. Would she be happy I was visiting, or would she find it stalkerish? Who visits someone in a foreign country without an invitation?

By the time I had landed she found me on Facebook and sent me a message.

"So... I'm coming to Bucharest in a week," I said.

I waited. I could see that she was typing and was nervous.

She was stunned but happy.

It was a cold night in Bucharest when I first

saw her. She had just gotten off of work and was bundled in a scarf and jacket. I moved in to kiss her and was deftly guided to her cheek. We went to dinner and chatted like normal, making no mention of the thwarted kiss.

The next couple days went about the same. I'd entertain myself during the day, meet her after work, try to kiss her, be politely denied, do something fun in Bucharest with her, and be refused again when saying goodbye.

One night she and her sister spent all day making me an amazing Romanian dinner. I can best describe the main dish as a delicious casserole made of garlic bread and chicken, and the dessert was way more cake than we could possibly eat. I was really touched by their hospitality, especially as I had shown up on my own initiative and was spending time with Lucia every day.

I tried one last time to kiss her and, when rejected, expressed that I thought she was just being shy, but that I wouldn't persist if she didn't want me to kiss her. She said that she didn't, so I dropped it.

We still spent time together. That weekend we went to see her favorite castle (Peleş) in Brasov, and Transylvania. We spent the night in a hotel and conspicuously slept as far from each other as possible on the bed. Despite being shoved into the friend zone, I liked her more and more. I admired how positive she was, how much she loved her country, and how quick-witted she was.

On the train ride back I mentioned that I had
read that Edison taught his second wife Morse
code so that they could tap messages to each
other. She suggested that we do the same, so
we learned Morse code together, quizzing each
other by tapping each other's legs. At one point
she looked me in the eyes and I was quite sure
she wanted me to kiss her. But I was tired of
being shut down and had told her I was going
to stop trying, so I let the moment pass.

Before I knew it it was my last day in Romania.
The ten days had gone by quickly, and there
was more of Romania that I wanted to see. The
country had lived up to the hype and I enjoyed
Lucia's company even more than I had expected
to.

I had one final dinner with her and her sister
and we walked to the train station to say our
goodbyes. Just as Lucia was about to go
through the fare gate I suggested that she
come back to my hotel and play gin rummy with
me. She agreed.

We played gin rummy, and then she beat me at
poker, and then she kissed me. We stayed up
the entire night talking. At one point she said
something like, "I would have never guessed we
had so much in common."

My first reaction was that we didn't have much
in common, but then as I thought about it, I
realized we did. And I realized that I liked her

and wanted to date her even though she lived about as far away as a person could get. She rode with me in the taxi to the airport in the morning. We said our goodbyes and I watched her walk out of the airport before going through security.

From then on we talked twice a day. There were two overlaps in our time zones, one of us was always going to bed as the other was waking up. We'd talk for a couple hours and then go to sleep looking forward to waking up to a message from the other. It was a nice rhythm. We talked about future trips we'd go on, how great our time together was, and visits we'd make to see the other person.

And then, one day, something was different. It's hard to pinpoint exactly what, but when you talk to someone twice a day you become hyper-sensitive to the subtleties of their communication. I could tell that I had lost her, probably to some guy who wasn't so far away. We continued to speak for a while, but the wind had left our sails.

Out of frustration I told her I couldn't talk to her anymore. It was too distracting. Two months later I changed my mind, but she wouldn't reply to me. That was two years ago, and my once-every-six-month messages have gone unanswered.

And More
Written in Maui

These are just a few of the people I've met in the past eight or so years of traveling. For every person I've written about here, there are dozens of others who I've met whose interactions don't quite warrant a story.

Just last week I was in Fiji and was offered a ride, soda, and cookies by a police officer. I took the ride and declined the refreshments. He dropped me off near a swimming hole I was going to, and there I found a couple Fijians helping all the tourists with the rope swing. When someone jumped and it went out of reach, they'd jump from the rocks to grab it. I watched this for a little while and came to the conclusion that they must either be leading a tour or work there.

But then I talked to one of the guys and he laughed and said they just live nearby and just liked to swim there. This isn't an interesting enough story to be a chapter in the book, but it's very typical of what I've experienced around the world. Most of the kindness and positive interactions I've had have been unremarkable apart from the fact that they collectively reinforce my faith in humanity.

There's plenty of serendipity and human kindness back at home, too, but it's not quite the same as that found when traveling. People all around the world want you to have a good time when you visit their city, and they go out of their way to ensure it. And those who travel tend to be more outgoing and open to making friends as they travel, so you end up sharing adventures with people whom you'd never otherwise get to know.

I hope you've enjoyed the stories of the adventures I've shared with strangers around the world, and I hope that you go out there and make your own stories. All I takes is a willingness to step just slightly outside of your comfort zone.